Just Around the Corner, in New Jersey

Just Around the Corner, in New Jersey

by Edward Brown

THE MIDDLE ATLANTIC PRESS
Wilmington, Delaware

Published by
The Middle Atlantic Press, Inc.
848 Church Street
Wilmington, Delaware 19899
text © 1984 by Edward Brown
drawings © 1984 by Robert Sebbo
ISBN 0-912608-17-X
Manufactured in the United States of America

Library of Congress Cataloging in Publication Data

Brown, Edward, 1931–
    Just around the corner, in New Jersey.

    Summary: A collection of stories based on notable
events and people in New Jersey.
    1. New Jersey—History—Anecdotes, facetiae, satire,
etc.—Juvenile literature.   [1. New Jersey—History]
I. Title.
F134.3.B76   1984   974.9   83-23653
ISBN 0-912608-17-X

This book is for my patient wife

Contents

Foreword

My brothers and I were lucky enough to have a father who loved to tell stories, and he had many good ones to tell: memories of the wild days in a jazz band at the University of Pennsylvania in the Roaring Twenties; the challenge of building mighty locomotives at the Baldwin Works between college terms; his first delivery of a baby in the pitch black of a farmhouse as a young doctor.

Unlike other physicians of his day he didn't laugh at folk remedies, and he was intrigued by the supernatural and stories which ended in questions, rather than conclusions.

We lived in a house which had been built a century before. A couple of generations had lived and died there. The house shifted oddly now and again, as if trying to throw off an unhappy memory, and there were unexplained noises in the dark.

My father claimed that often after midnight, when he was working alone in his study, he could hear ghosts beginning to move around in the old house. Flames in the fireplace would suddenly flare up, and his cat would arch her back with fear and crowd close to his knees, but dad liked having ghosts for company.

So it's not surprising that of all his stories, tales of things which creaked in the night were his favorites, especially "The Red Scarf."

He'd heard this strange story while in medical school. The professor who told him the story said it was true, that it had happened to him.

For some reason, in our family Christmas was the time for ghost stories, and no Christmas was complete for us three boys until the mysterious tale of the little girl with the red scarf was retold.

People have been living in this old state of New Jersey for a long time—restless Europeans in search of something better since the 17th century, and the Indians before them. All sorts of things have happened here, both good and bad, and some of the stories in this book are about those interesting events, and people, *JUST AROUND THE CORNER* in our part of the world.

From the Shadows

The Red Scarf

A woman dreams of a plane crash and begs her husband not to take the business flight he had planned. Next day, the plane goes down in flames. A man has a vision of a mighty ship smashing into a floating mountain. A week later, the Titanic, the world's largest ship, hits an iceberg and sinks. A dead child's laughter is heard in the sunroom where she used to play.

Things like this happen, though we can't explain them. They're outside the ordinary, part of something called the "supernatural."

Doctors, who deal with life and death almost every day, often run up against strange situations in which reason seems to play no part. One such experience was had by a doctor practicing in Camden many years ago. It was midwinter, and a deadly disease was sweeping the city. This was before effective cures had been found for viruses, and people were dying of the 'flu. The only cure was rest and careful medical attention. Sometimes, this wasn't enough.

Here's the doctor's story:

"It seemed half the people in town were sick with this 'flu and every doctor in town was working very hard to save as many people as he could. I was young, but I'd been hard at work at the hospital all day, and I was dead tired. All I wanted was a good dinner and some rest."

"I'd eaten and was on my way upstairs when I passed by the hall window and looked out. There, in the snow, stood a small girl looking up at my window. By the gas lamp, I noticed she had on a red scarf and hat. She stood quietly, just looking up."

"'Something's wrong,' I said to myself. 'She needs help.' I went down the stairs, picked up my medical bag,

13

put on my coat, and went outside."

"The girl was still there. 'Doctor,' she said, 'you must come. My mother is sick and needs you.' Her eyes shone strangely as she spoke, and I could not say no. I was tired, but I was a doctor."

"I took the little girl by the hand and let her lead me through the dark streets. It was a bitter night. The wind off the Delaware River roared down Cooper Street and the snow blew into a white mist that was everywhere."

"The little girl's hand was deathly cold. She said nothing, but guided me to a rundown tenement building about half a mile away."

"We went in and up the stairs to the second floor. The little girl's cold hand left mine. 'There,' she said, pointing to a door. 'My mother's in there.' The odd shine in her eyes was back again."

"As I entered the room, I noticed the girl going into the room next door. I was still wondering about her, but for the next few hours I was too busy trying to help her mother. The girl had been right; her mother was very sick and weak."

"I fought with the forces of death for her life, and finally the long night was over. She was still weak, but she would live. I breathed a prayer of thanks."

"When she came to herself, this worn-looking woman looked at me in surprise and said, 'Doctor, how did you get here? How did you know I needed you? There was no one . . .'"

"'But didn't you send your daughter to bring me, the little girl in the red scarf and hat?' I asked. Her eyes opened wide at this. 'Doctor, that cannot be. My little girl died of the 'flu yesterday morning. She's in that room there,' she said, indicating a side door."

"Thoughts tumbling in my mind, I opened the door and walked into the next room. After my eyes grew accustomed to the grey dawn light, I saw a small figure lying on a bed. It was a young girl, her arms crossed in death over her chest. On a nearby table, neatly folded, lay a red scarf and hat."

"I bent down and looked at her closely and a quick chill ran up my back. There was no doubt about it, this was the same girl who had brought me here to her mother a few hours earlier."

"Now I began to understand the cold hands and the odd shine in her eyes, but my understanding ended there. How was the whole thing possible? Could a child's love be so great that she could somehow make her way through the dark shadow of death to help her mother live?"

"I don't know the answer, but I'm an old man now, and I've been thinking about this all my life. Maybe one day soon I'll find out."

In the Sweet By and By

A boy and girl walk along the dunes on Long Beach Island, turning their faces from the sharpness of the wind. It's close to Christmas and the last of the fall northeast storms is just now blowing itself out. The beach is cold, but at the end of this winter stroll there will be a hot drink and a warm fireside for the young couple.

The wind drops, and there's a curious pause in the pounding of the surf for a moment. In the sudden silence, the young people are surprised by the sound of singing, somewhere out past the breakers.

Yes, there's no doubt about it, that's what it is, a woman's voice singing an old hymn or what could be a lullaby. The two run to the edge of the water and strain their eyes to peer through the dusk out to sea. Nothing.

The wind rises once more, the surf breaks in again, and the singing is drowned out. But was it singing, or just some strange trick of the wind and water on the winter beach?

The young couple walk home puzzled, but if they were to ask oldtimers on Long Beach Island about this odd experience, they might hear a story which would make them even more confused.

It all goes back to 1822, when a driving winter storm had wrecked a sailing ship, the *Tolck*, on a sandbar off Long Beach Island. Life-saving crews worked all day to get the passengers and crew off the ship, which was going to pieces in the heavy seas as night began to fall.

By then only four people remained on board the *Tolck*—the captain, his wife, their baby girl, and the ship's first mate. Rescuers could only make one more trip before dark. Only one or perhaps two people would get off the ship that night.

16

The captain urged his wife to leave with the baby. She looked at her husband's desperate face and made her decision—come what may, she would stay by his side. She kissed her child and put her into the arms of the first mate. He would make the last trip and see the baby safely ashore.

To calm the frightened child, the captain's wife began to sing a hymn, "In the Sweet By and By." The soothing lullaby did calm the child, and the sound of the mother's singing was the last thing the mate heard as he went over the side into the lifeboat with the baby.

The captain lashed himself and his wife to the main-mast that terrible night to wait until dawn for rescue . . . They were found next morning in each other's arms, dead from cold and exhaustion.

The child was sent to be raised by relatives in New York, grew up there, married and had her own children. The tragic end of the *Tolck* and her captain and his wife seemed to be forgotten.

Why then are there those on Long Beach Island who will swear they have heard a woman's soft voice singing an old lullaby when the storms and heavy seas tear at the shore?

Is it something unexplained out of the past, an anguished mother trying to calm her terrified baby, giving the child some last sound of a loving mother's voice?

Or is it nothing beyond the sound of the sea and the wind?

Joe Hooker Keeps His Promise

"I don't see how we ever made it," Joe said to his wife, Milly.

She smiled as they both breathed the air of freedom for the first time in their lives. "If the Underground Railway had not helped us, we'd still be on the plantation in Georgia."

Joe Hooker and his wife were runaway slaves. The time was 1859, more than one hundred years ago, and slavery was still permitted in the American South, but not in the northern states. There were many who believed that slavery was wrong, and these people did what they could to help slaves escape to the North on the famous Underground Railway.

Joe and Milly were on their way to Canada. There the two would be safe and free—nobody could make them return to a life of slavery.

But they were not safe yet. Milly looked out over the flat landscape of South Jersey. An orange moon was rising in the east. It did not look very different from Georgia. She shivered. "Yes, but we'll still have to be careful. Remember what our friend, Mr. Davis, said about that gang of slave hunters here in Mt. Herndon."

Joe frowned and replied, "You're right. We don't want these bounty hunters to catch hold of us. We'll have to stay well hidden in this wagon shed until tomorrow night. Then Mr. Davis should be able to get us further along to the next Underground Railway station . . . let's get some sleep."

The runaway couple lay down to rest. What they didn't know was that they had already been seen. Even as they talked in low voices in the shed, men were circling the building and creeping up on them in the darkening night.

They were members of the gang Mr. Davis had told Milly and Joe about, cruel and dangerous men who kept a sharp eye out for runaway slaves. If they succeeded in capturing the runaways, they could send them back to their masters for a reward. Sometimes, if the runaways they caught were too troublesome and hard to handle, the gang would hang them. This had happened near here.

The gang burst into the shed. They had torches and shotguns. Joe awoke at once and began to fight the men. He was strong from years of working in the fields and he fought hard. It would be terrible to be sent back to slavery after coming this far.

But finally Joe was beaten. He was thrown to the floor and chained. As he was dragged out of the shed, Joe called to his wife, "Run, Milly, run!" His sobbing wife ran off into the darkness. Before the startled men knew what was happening, she was gone in the night.

The gang was furious. Half their reward was gone with Milly. The leader decided to teach this runaway a lesson.

"You'll pay for that!" shouted the angry leader. The men hustled Joe over to a large oak tree. A rope whistled over a lower branch of the tree, a noose on one end, and on the other, a dozen of the gang ready to haul Joe up to his death.

Joe knew then he was going to die. He looked at the now silent men around him. Because it was dark, he could see only their glittering eyes. He made a promise to himself.

The orange moon rode high in the sky now. In the last moments of his life, Joe pointed overhead with his chained hands. "I swear on that moon to be back. You can kill me, but I'll be back. I promise you that you'll see me again."

A chill ran through the men at the foot of the tree as

Joe died. No runaway had ever said anything like this before. What could he mean?

Joe was buried that night near the oak tree. Nothing more was heard of his wife. The incident seemed closed.

Then, at the time of the next full moon, strange things began to happen. A dark figure was seen swinging from the oak tree. People heard the clanking of chains near the shed, and some claimed they heard a man's voice calling, "Milly, Milly."

People grew frightened. One night two months after Joe was hanged, a light was seen in the wagon shed. The gang leader who had killed Joe boldly went into the shed to show he wasn't afraid. There was no one there, but as the man turned to leave, he saw a pair of eyes staring at him out of the darkness. Terrified now, he jumped on his horse and galloped away, determined to put as much distance between himself and the wagon shed as he could.

Next day, the gang leader's horse was found in its stall, but he was missing. His friends found him by the side of a bridge, his neck broken. "A fall from his horse," people said.

But the word got around and the townsfolk of Mt. Herndon began to avoid the corner where the wagon shed stood. On those nights when a full moon rose in the sky, nobody would come near the place.

All this happened a long time ago. Yet, even today in this town, people still shun the spot where the old wagon shed once stood. They can't tell why, but there's something scary about that dark corner of town near the woods.

Nobody can say for sure, but Joe Hooker may still be keeping his promise.

An Old Inn with More than Memories

For years neighbors have sworn they've seen a ghost floating this way and that above the grounds, looking for something. Some say that the uneasy spirit of Peter Louderback may be trying to find the treasure he hid, to keep it from British troops during the American Revolution.

The story goes that Louderback, the wealthy owner of the Seven Stars Tavern in Woodstown, learned that a band of British soldiers was on the way to ransack his house. He and his servants quickly buried the gold and silver in the tavern garden. But in the excitement Louderback must have forgotten just where the treasure was buried, because after the British searched his house and left without finding the treasure, he couldn't find it either. Some say he's still looking for it.

Louderback's ghost is only one of many which are said to haunt this historic South Jersey landmark. The inn, now a private home, was once a bustling 18th century stagecoach stop. It must have been a very popular place in the old days, because people who were guests two hundred years ago keep coming back for visits.

Beside the treasure-hunting Louderback, there's the Hessian soldier. This man, a hired soldier fighting for the British, was badly wounded in a fight which took place near the inn. He was brought there to die, and every now and again is said to reappear in the tavern taproom, wringing his hands and moaning.

Then there is the Tory spy who was hanged from the window during the Revolution. He's been seen back there on occasion, under the eaves of the roof, in the attic, with a rope wrapped around his neck.

Stories about the Seven Stars go so far as to hint that one of the regular "haunts" of the old tavern may be the pirate Blackbeard himself.

Some accounts say that he was murdered near the Seven Stars. Blackbeard or whoever, people have seen something here on dark nights, something dressed in what looks like a pirate outfit, with its head held under one arm.

Then there's the woman with long hair. She was seen by one of the younger members of the family which now owns the Seven Stars. He awoke in the middle of the night with the feeling that someone was watching him. He looked up in the darkness from his bed and saw the figure of a woman with long, trailing hair floating a foot or two over him.

The present owners have picked up all sorts of old objects around the inn—parts of tools, ax heads, horseshoes, things like that—and one special object which may explain some of the ghostly activity at the Seven Stars: *a human skull.*

It may be true that Innkeeper Louderback is still searching for his lost treasure, but one of these days another ghost might be coming around looking for his head.

Yo, Ho, Ho on Barnegat Bay

When one thinks of pirates, pictures of the skull and crossbones and fierce men with swords come to mind. But not that long ago on the Jersey Shore there was a different sort of pirate. He got his booty not with cannonfire and swordplay, but with trickery.

In the bygone days of sailing ships, wicked men would use a trick to lure ships into shallow water—known as "shoals"—just off Barnegat Light. After the ships would strike bottom and begin to break up, the pirates would be waiting on shore for anything which might wash in.

When a storm was brewing, the Barnegat pirates would put a lantern on a mule and drive him up and down the beach. A ship's captain, out at sea, would see the moving light. He would think it was the lights of a ship in safe waters, and often would steer his vessel in that direction.

Of course, the ship would soon run herself up on the Barnegat Shoal and would begin to wreck. Whatever the ship was carrying—or some of it, anyway—would come ashore in the storm.

The story goes that one dark and stormy night a ship was sighted by the pirates just north of Barnegat Inlet. They loaded the mule with a bright lantern and walked him up and down the beach. On this night the daughter of the pirate leader was in charge of the ship wrecking, and she proved to be as good at it as her father.

The ship changed course and headed straight for the light and what the ship's captain thought to be safe waters. But his vessel soon struck, and in the raging storm was broken to pieces just offshore.

The cargo, silks and cloth in bales, came ashore. And then the drowned bodies of the sailors began washing up.

The pirates went from body to body, taking wallets, watches, rings—whatever was of value. The pirate leader's daughter did too, and she had gathered herself a handful of gold coins by robbing the bodies.

There was one to go, right in front of her. She heaved the sailor's body over and began to take a ring off the finger. Then she glanced at the face of the drowned seaman, and let out a terrible cry.

The surprised pirates watched her collapse over the body, sobbing and moaning. When they gathered around her, they understood. The dead sailor in the sand was her sweetheart, last seen six months ago before he left as first mate on a ship to England.

Disasters
and
Excitement

Hitting the Silk Over New Jersey

The famed U.S. Army paratroopers have a little known connection with New Jersey that goes all the way back to their formation.

In the summer of 1940, with World War II still more than a year away for the United States, the Army decided to organize a "test platoon" to develop training practices for larger groups of paratroopers.

We had no parachute troops at this point. But other countries, including Germany, had used them successfully, so it was felt necessary to keep up.

Forty-eight men and two officers, all volunteers, were picked for the test platoon. They at once began learning everything they needed to know about parachuting at Fort Benning, Georgia. They had a tough schedule of physical training, including constant running and frequent trips through the obstacle course.

Though the men were getting the feeling of a parachute landing by jumping out of the back of moving trucks, there was no way of finding out how they would react to actual parachuting.

What could be done to get them ready for the jump itself?

Then somebody remembered he had seen a parachute tower at the New York World's Fair. It was 150 feet high, was made of steel girders, and was as popular as the roller coaster as an amusement. Riders were hoisted to the top of the tower and then let down under a parachute with wires attached to it to slow the descent.

The World's Fair tower was owned by the Safe Parachute Company of Hightstown. They used it to test their own parachutes, and they had two towers operating at Hightstown. If the test platoon could use them, it would be a big step forward in their training.

After a long series of telephone calls, arrangements were made and the men of the test platoon were flown north to Fort Dix. They'd stay there for ten days while training on the Safe Parachute Company towers.

The men were surprised at the height of the towers, but got to work right away. They first made "jumps" using the parachute with wires attached. Then they went on to the second tower.

A jumper using this tower came close to making an actual parachute jump. He was strapped into a harness and lifted to the top of the tower, where he was released. There were no wires or other attachments. The parachute floated down freely, like the real thing, and the parachutist had to do a good landing when he came into contact with Mother Earth.

After the towers only one thing more remained to be done—the jump itself, from an airplane. The group went back to Fort Benning, but before they jumped themselves, a demonstration was put on for them.

The test platoon had not yet actually seen anyone make a parachute jump from an airplane. They gathered to watch a dummy dropped from a circling plane. To everyone's horror, the dummy's parachute did not open! An instructor quickly explained that a soldier, not a dummy, could have saved himself by pulling the ripcord on his reserve parachute.

During the final week of training, the men of the test platoon made their jumps and became the first American paratroopers.

Digging Mr. Lincoln's Tunnel

It was 1934 and the Great Depression had settled over the country like a dark cloud. There were too few jobs and too many takers for the jobs there were. Bread lines and soup kitchens were set up to hand out food to the hungry. People by the thousands lost their homes because they could not pay the rent or the mortgage. Life was grim.

When the announcement was made in the spring that work would begin on the Lincoln Tunnel connecting New Jersey and New York, it was no surprise that job applicants showed up in droves.

Plans called for a great steel box, a "caisson," to be lowered to the riverbed of the Hudson. There was an airtight wall above the bottom of the caisson, which had a cutting edge on it.

Workmen would go through the airlock above the face of the caisson and dig into the mud and clay. To keep the mud and water out of the working space, air had to be pumped in at great pressure, four times, in fact, the normal pressure of sea level.

The digging itself was hard, dirty, and dangerous. Because of the great air pressure at the face, the men working there had to be in good physical shape. No one with heart, lung, or ear trouble could stand the harsh working conditions.

The "sandhogs," as these men called themselves, faced the constant danger of blow-outs. A blow-out could come about when the air under pressure in the caisson suddenly shot out through a pocket in the mud. The pressure was lost, and the workers could be trapped with nothing to keep back the water and muck.

Another danger which faced the sandhogs was the

chance of getting the "bends." Men working under several times the normal amount of pressure have a great deal of nitrogen in their bodies. If they don't undergo a gradual return to normal air pressure in a decompression chamber they can be in trouble. Instead of leaving the body slowly, the nitrogen forms in bubbles and froth near the joints, causing great pain. If a bubble reaches the heart, death is immediate.

But despite the dangers of blow-outs, cave-ins, and the bends, the men hired to build the tunnel considered themselves lucky; they had jobs.

And the work went on, with the caissons pushed toward each other under the Hudson River from the New York and New Jersey sides. They met and joined a year after the first construction started.

Two and one half years later, the Lincoln Tunnel opened to traffic: 20,000 cubic yards of concrete in the roadway, a fourteen inch cement lining around the inside, 60,000 miles of wiring, and one million squares of tile in the ceiling.

The baseball great, Babe Ruth, was on hand to make the opening speech, as were hundreds of officials, and a huge crowd of ordinary citizens.

Many of the men who built the Lincoln Tunnel were also there, and they rightfully stood proud that day. But the tunnel had used up more than hundreds of tons of steel and concrete, and thousands of hours of sweat. It had taken the lives of men—eight of them—and they were among the missing at the gala opening celebration.

Martians in the Marshes

People couldn't believe their ears, and they certainly didn't want to: creatures from Mars landing in a cornfield near Trenton?

But that was what the radio announcer had said, on this fall night in 1938. According to continued reports, something which was at first thought to be a meteorite had landed on a farm in Grover's Mill.

But this one was like no other meteorite which had dropped out of space onto earth. Shortly after it landed, a number of cylinder-like machines came out of the meteorite, now identified as a space ship.

As an excited crowd pressed in closer to see what was going to happen, laser beams shot out of the Martian machines and drove them back.

From then on, all the news was bad. Flashes from excited newscasters interrupting a musical program came one after another, each more frightening than the last.

"Soldiers with rifles and machine guns surrounded the Martians. The machines exploded with bursts of fire and 7,000 men were dead . . . the machines began their march north to New York . . . Army aircraft tried to bomb them and instead were themselves shot out of the sky by heat rays . . . reports came in of other Martian landings in Buffalo, Chicago, St. Louis . . . as they got into the city, the Martians began using poison gas to kill earth people" . . . the tone of the newscasters was hysterical as "the Martians moved up Broadway" . . . then there was silence.

And the people listening got hysterical, too. They were taking seriously what was supposed to be a pre-Halloween joke by actor-director Orson Welles.

Welles had adapted an 1898 science-fiction story, *War of the Worlds,* to modern times. He substituted fake radio reports for the passages in the book which described the invasion of earth by the Martians.

But he did it too well, and thousands of people within broadcast range of the *CBS Mercury Theater of the Air* in New York were convinced that the Martians had arrived. Terrified people thought their last moments on earth were at hand.

There was panic. The roads leading from New York were jammed with people fleeing into South Jersey, away from the city. Hospitals treated scores of people for shock. The switchboard of the *New York Times* was flooded with calls asking if the report of Martian landings was true. Townsfolk in smaller cities demanded power companies turn off the electricity so the Martians would miss them in the dark. Churches were clogged with praying people, and families hurriedly equipped themselves with homemade gas masks to save themselves from the Martian "poison fog."

Eventually the word got out that the radio broadcasts were all a hoax, that there were no Martian invaders with lasers or poison gas, that there was nothing to panic over. Never before had there been a time when the phrase, "Nothing to fear but fear itself" applied so aptly.

And probably most of those who panicked missed Orson Welles' final words on his "War of the Worlds" bombshell broadcast on Halloween Eve. He said the program was "The Mercury Theater's own way of dressing up in a sheet . . . and saying BOO!"

Next day—and for some time after that—Orson Welles had some explaining to do.

Death in the Orchard

The bodies, both shot through the head, were found in an orchard across the river from New Brunswick by a couple of youngsters out looking for mushrooms. The man was identified as the Reverend Edward W. Hall, Rector of the largest church in New Brunswick. The woman's body was that of Mrs. Eleanor Mills, a member of the church who sang in the choir and often assisted the minister in his visits to the sick and the poor. But now they were both dead, lying side by side in a lonely orchard. It was early fall, 1922.

The clues were few, and the police were baffled. There was no weapon found with the bodies, although a number of people said they heard cries and shots coming from the orchard the night before. What the police *did* find was a litter of paper around the bodies, including some notes written by Mrs. Mills which seemed to show that the choir singer was in love with the minister.

They raised a very difficult and delicate question. Perhaps Mrs. Hall, the minister's wife, or Mr. Mills, the choir singer's husband, had a motive for the murder? The police questioned them both, but found no evidence to support that theory, or any other theory. In fact, after a while, there weren't any more theories and puzzled police went down one blind alley after another in the case.

The unsolved murders became a national sensation. Even *The New York Times*, probably the most important newspaper in the country, got into the act. It suggested that powerful politicians and wealthy community leaders were deliberately covering up evidence in the crime.

Then, two months after the killings, Clifton Hayes, 18, was arrested and charged with the crime on the evidence of a man named Raymond Schneider. Schneider

said that Hayes had confessed to him that he had mistaken the two victims for another couple—his girlfriend and someone else—and had killed them in a jealous rage.

But Schneider fell apart under police questioning and soon admitted he'd made up the whole story. He got two years in prison for perjury as a result.

Four years later, something else: Arthur S. Reihl claimed that when his wife had been a maid at the Hall home, she had been paid off to stay quiet about "what she knew about the killing."

She denied this, and police were again at a dead end in the Hall/Mills murder case.

Then, in 1926, Mrs. Hall was finally arrested and charged with the murder of her husband and Mrs. Mills. But nothing came of this, and the case remained open.

That was over half a century ago. The mystery of the two bodies in the orchard is still unsolved. Who did it? A jealous wife or husband? A hired killer? Was the fate of these two simply the result of an unlucky meeting with an armed maniac who had murder on his mind?

Nobody knows, except the killer, if he's still around a lifetime later. He—or she—got away with it.

The Great Sled Raid

It was the dark winter of 1779–80, the sixth winter of the American War for Independence, and the harshest winter anyone could remember.

Washington's army was camped at Jockey Hollow, near Morristown. Trying to survive in snows five feet deep and winds which howled like devils was pure misery. The soldiers' spirit was cracking.

Something had to be done before the American Army fell apart completely. What was needed was a victory to give hope to the American cause.

One of Washington's generals, William Alexander, came up with a plan. British forces were dug in for the winter on Staten Island, not far from Jockey Hollow, and the open water between Staten Island and New Jersey was frozen solid. Why not try a surprise raid on the British, to capture some prisoners and perhaps shake them up a bit?

General Washington agreed, and in the cold pre-dawn of January 15th, hundreds of sleds were drawn up just in front of the American lines, opposite Staten Island.

Soon, American troops were speeding across the frozen surface of Arthur Kill on their way to Staten Island. The plan was that their sudden appearance out of the dark west would completely surprise the British.

In the words of one American soldier who was there, "the weather was cold enough to cut a man in two." Certainly the British would not be expecting an attack on such a bitter night.

But spies were everywhere at this time, and word of the American plans had reached the British headquarters on Staten Island. Though the first attack of the Americans drove the British outposts back, the main body of troops held. Then a British ship, locked for the winter in the ice within cannon range, began shelling the American raiding force.

General Alexander called the attack off and marched his men back to Jockey Hollow with some captured hay and a few British prisoners. The British followed them and for a time it looked as if the Americans might not get safely back to their own lines. They lost some of their own men as prisoners to the British, but most of the Americans managed to return to Jockey Hollow.

The "Great Sled Raid" was a failure. In fact, a few days later the British on Staten Island went on a raid of their own, burned a number of American buildings and captured more prisoners.

But the most serious casualty of the raid was General Alexander himself. The long and anxious hours in the snow and the disappointing results, came close to breaking the fifty-four year old general's spirit. He could no longer stand the strain of battle. He never again took an active role in the struggle for American freedom.

At First, the Ball Was Round

There were fifty players on the field, the ball was round, and they made up the rules as they went along. But it was still the first intercollegiate football game in the United States, and it was played between Rutgers and Princeton.

On November 6, 1869, young men from these two New Jersey colleges met in New Brunswick for the first of three football challenge matches.

The students themselves had arranged the games. There were no cheerleaders, marching bands, or even uniforms, although the Rutgers players did wear red headbands.

The playing field in back of the Rutgers gymnasium was about the same size as a football field of today, but that was about all that was the same.

In this early version of football there was no need of fast running backs. The object was to pass and kick the ball downfield, then boot it through the goals for a score.

Even though the twenty-five players on each side wore no equipment, the game was rough. Instead of timed quarters to limit the game, it would be over when the first team won by scoring six goals.

Compared to football of today, this first intercollegiate game resembled a cross between rugby and soccer.

The game began at 3:00 o'clock and the first goal went almost immediately to Rutgers. Princeton had tried a surprise long kick and the ball got loose. Rutgers jumped on it, and, in a series of short dribbles, got the ball to the team captains near the goal for a quick score.

The Princeton captain, William S. Gummere, told one of his strongest players, "Big Mike," to break up the Rutgers interference. He drove into the massed Rutgers players and scattered them. Princeton got the ball and made its first score.

But Rutgers had a trick up its sleeve. This was freshman Madison Ball, who could run in the same direction as the ball, then step over it and pass it back to another teammate. While the Princeton players were trying to figure out how he did it, Ball passed to one of his captains and Rutgers scored again.

Then it was "Big Mike" again for Princeton. He muscled the ball away from Rutgers and, surrounded by a screen of his teammates, tied the score.

The next two goals went to Rutgers. During this interval something happened which spectators remembered almost as well as they recalled the scores themselves. "Big Mike" and a large Rutgers player collided head on in a wild scramble for the ball. They smashed into a fence, but neither was hurt. However, there is no way of knowing what happened to the fence.

Another noteworthy incident which could have changed the outcome of the game occurred when a Rutgers player who had been hit in the head once too often took the ball and almost scored against his own team! Rutgers players blocked his kick.

But then Princeton came back to erase the two goal lead Rutgers had built up.

The score was now four goals all, and the crowd was going wild. Two goals more and the game would be over.

The Rutgers field captain, William J. Leggett, came up with a new tactic. He'd noticed that Princeton had been using the greater height of its biggest players to keep the ball over the heads of the shorter Rutgers men. He told his players to keep the ball on the ground, or as close to it as they could.

This worked, and a heartened Rutgers team stormed down the field for two more goals—and became the winner of the nation's first college football game, played, appropriately enough, between two of America's oldest colleges.

Rutgers and Princeton started something on that fall afternoon in 1869. Within ten years, college football was on its way to developing into an institution. Today, it's hard to imagine Saturday afternoons in the autumn without college football.

And it all goes back to fifty enthusiastic young men in high button shoes on a muddy field in New Brunswick.

Hitting Back

The United States had been at war for almost a year—and victory was far away. The Second World War had burst upon a country struggling to recover from the Great Depression. Going from the bread line to the firing line took some getting used to—and some time.

But the Civil Air Patrol, organized in New Jersey a week before Pearl Harbor and spreading nationwide soon after, was already off the ground and running.

The Civil Air Patrol began flying over Jersey coastal waters during the spring of 1942, when German submarines were having a field day sinking American vessels from Maine to Florida. CAP pilots would radio in positions of ships going down and send the Coast Guard after survivors.

Sometimes these civilian pilots would come upon surfaced German U-boats, their crews taking the sun on deck. The sailors would wave and laugh: they knew the CAP aircraft were unarmed and presented no threat.

When this happened, CAP pilots would grind their teeth in rage. They wanted more than anything to hit back. Then someone high up suggested it might be a good idea to arm CAP airplanes on the chance that one might get a shot at a visiting German submarine.

The tide was about to turn for the U-boats, and one of the first indications of this came when armed CAP planes began patrolling out of a new base in Atlantic City.

Wynant Farr, Al Muthrig, and John Haggin flew the first mission from Atlantic City, and tucked under the wings of their Grumman Widgeon they had a pair of 325-pound depth charges just in case.

Fifteen minutes out, in the middle of reporting the sinking of a torpedoed tanker, the three heard over the radio that another CAP aircraft had sighted a German sub 25 miles from their position.

The Widgeon headed for the sighting at full throttle, low over the water, but when they got there, no sub was to be seen on the surface.

But soon the CAP pilots made out a dark shape moving slowly forward in the shallow waters of the Continental Shelf. A sharp thrill of excitement ran through them: the enemy, and they were going to get their chance for first blood.

The Widgeon had a large fuel capacity, and the pilots took full advantage of it, circling and tracking the U-boat for a full four hours before the German commander came up to periscope depth for a look-see.

This was what the CAP pilots had been waiting for. The depth charges carried by the Widgeon were set for shallow detonation, and Haggin made his approach from behind, lining up the airplane on the trailing wake of the periscope.

Dry-mouthed, hearts pounding, a couple of over-age businessmen and a paper box manufacturer were going to war. The Grumman roared in, one thousand feet above the water. Farr, using a homemade bombsight, released the first depth charge.

As the plane banked, the CAP men looked back to see the massive charge explode just ahead of the sub. The U-boat's bow was thrown up out of the sea, and she immediately began to crash dive—or sink.

The second depth charge, directly over a spreading oil slick, brought more oil and some debris to the surface. The Widgeon circled and still more oil and debris bubbled up.

It was a kill, one of the two confirmed sinkings and several probables CAP was to be credited with in the next 18 months.

It wasn't all one-sided, though. Ninety CAP aircraft went down, and 26 pilots lost their lives in anti-submarine patrolling off the coast. And they weren't even in the Army.

City Up Against the Wall

The match which lighted the fires was the arrest of a cab driver by Newark police for a traffic violation. At his bail hearing for resisting arrest, he said he had been beaten by the officers.

It was the second week in July in the hot summer of 1967. Conditions in rundown Newark had gotten themselves into such a state that people were wondering *when*—not *if*—the big trouble was going to start.

Newark had the most crime per 100,000 people in the United States, the heaviest per person tax burden, and one of the highest rates of infant death in the country. Fifteen percent of its citizens were without jobs, and Newark ranked seventh among major American cities in the number of drug addicts prowling the streets.

The sparks were there, and when word of the alleged beating got around, a protest meeting was held across the street from the Fourth Precinct Station.

Though civil rights leaders stressed the need to "cool it," things got out of hand almost as soon as the angry crowd gathered.

Rocks broke the station windows, and police, charging out to deal with the disturbance, were driven back inside by a hail of stones. Two homemade fire bombs burst against the side of the building.

In the heat of late evening, in the steam coming up from the grimy streets, the anger of the inner city people spilled over. Out of rage, frustration, and a deep sense of somehow having been cheated out of the good things of life, the poor of Newark's ghettos went wild.

What followed the next six days was looting, burning, "trashing," and death.

The stores on Seventeenth Street, near the Fourth

Precinct Police Station, were the first to be hit. It spread to Belmont, and the night was filled with the sounds of breaking glass and burglar alarms going off.

The police came out in force, but could not control the looting, so they tried a new tactic. They would try to contain the rioters and the damage along Seventeenth and Belmont, closing off the area and blocking streets into it.

By very early morning, just before dawn, the rioters ran out of steam. Most simply went home, many to the Hayes Home Projects nearby. The riot was over; police and Newark officials almost cried with relief.

But it wasn't over. Another demonstration was scheduled by community leaders for the Fourth Precinct area on the next evening, Thursday. People gathered and an Afro drum group began pounding out rhythm. A detective stood on the steps of the precinct station and asked the people to go home. Bottles and rocks came out of the crowd. People began knocking out the windows with sticks—it looked like things were going to be just like the night before.

It was worse. The looting began again, and this time it spread. Springfield Avenue went; rioters hassled passing motorists, and hundreds of people struggled to carry off stolen television sets, radios, and even refrigerators.

By Friday morning four hundred and fifty people were in jail, hundreds were injured, and five lay dead. Fourteen hundred policemen, all that Newark had, were out on the streets trying to put down what was being described as a "rebellion," and they couldn't do it.

Things were getting completely out of hand, and the Mayor of Newark requested help from the New Jersey National Guard. The Governor agreed, and later that morning the troops began rolling in.

Three thousand Guardsmen, along with five hundred

State Troopers, joined the Newark Police in the struggle. Just about everybody on both sides was scared, and there were ugly incidents.

Complete unfamiliarity with the city, the fear of rooftop snipers, and being kept on the move for days without rest, made some of the Guardsmen trigger-happy enough to shoot at shadows.

The nervous Guardsmen and the rampaging mobs made a bad mix. Later, there were claims that the introduction of this military force with its armored personnel carriers, machine guns and bayonetted rifles, made things worse rather than better.

It's certain the "revolt" didn't end when the troops showed up on Friday morning. From then until Monday afternoon, a "weekend war" was fought between roaming bands of rioters, mostly young men, and groups of patrolling soldiers.

Those who were there say that this "weekend war" was the worst of the whole nightmare. The center of Newark looked and sounded like an urban battlefield. Machine guns were rattling, people were screaming, there were flames from burning buildings, and the sound of sirens was everywhere. Nineteen people died between Friday dawn and Monday afternoon.

That Monday, the 17th, it ended. The anger died down, people got tired of the looting and the destruction, or maybe they just wanted to pick up their lives where they had left off the week before. But Newark wouldn't be the same again for a long time.

The Cry Was, "Poor Man's Blood in a Rich Man's War"

The Newark riots of 1967 were bad enough, but were nothing compared to the violent anti-draft protests more than one hundred years earlier in the city across the river.

It was July 1863 and the American Civil War, which would claim over one million dead before it ended, was still dividing the country. The end could be near, however. Lee's forces were on the march to Gettysburg for a do-or-die battle, to break the will of the Union Army.

Men were badly needed and the army had run short of volunteers. A draft law was passed, but it was unpopular, and those unwilling to serve did what they could to avoid it.

One way was to hire a "substitute" who would take the place of the man called up for service. This cost $300, a year's salary in those days.

A flood of immigrants was coming into the United States at this time, chiefly at New York, and many were finding they had arrived just in time to be drafted for the Civil War.

This went down badly. Nobody wanted to begin his new life by fighting in a war as soon as he stepped ashore.

Feeling against the draft grew, and in mid-July, 1863, a mob wrecked the offices of the Provost Marshall in New York City. The rioters not only smashed up the offices, they also burned the lists containing the names of 1,200 New Yorkers who had just been selected for service by the draft.

The rampage was on, and for the next three days the

city was in the hands of a mass of people who had gone crazy.

The draft office on Broadway was burned next, and then the mob broke into the homes of wealthy families on Lexington Avenue. Stores were looted, and offices and churches—even an orphanage—were burned.

The mob caught thirty police and government officials the first couple of days and hanged, shot, or kicked them to death, dancing and singing around the bodies.

The Police Commissioner of New York tried to calm the rioters by speaking to them. It was almost the last time he ever said anything to anybody. They dragged him through the gutter, beat him, and left him for dead in a horse trough. He survived, but barely.

By this time there were between 50,000 and 70,000 people involved. They had gotten hold of guns and were shooting at police and Home Guards from the upper windows of office buildings.

There were fights everywhere between groups of rioters and police and soldiers. The *Times* and *Tribune* newspaper offices were wrecked, and barricades went up on Eighth Avenue and on First Avenue.

A couple of artillery pieces were brought up on Second Avenue and Thirty-fourth, and police fired grapeshot to clear the area of rioters.

Troops were now on the way from the Battle of Gettysburg, but even battalions of infantry flooding New York City found they had trouble putting down the mob.

Put it down they did, however, and when the smoke cleared and the people came to their senses and went back to their homes, the cost was added up—ruined buildings, debris-laden streets, and twelve hundred people dead.

Glass Damage Exceeds a Million;
Few Downtown Buildings Escape

Insurance Companies ...

Sparks from Small Blaze Reach Explosives— Firemen Trapped.

CITY IS TERROR-STRICKEN

Great Part of Population Rushes to Streets, Many in Night Attire, Seeking Safety.

RIVER BRIDGES TREMBLE

Cars Crossing Lose Windows. All Police Called to Pro...

WO MEN UNDER ARREST

...arge of High Explosive Alleged to Have Been Moored Against Orders.

87 CARS OF SHELLS FIRED

Heavy Damage in Manhattan and Brooklyn—Statue of Liberty Hit.

The terrifying explosion in and near the National Storage Company's plant on Black Tom Island, Jersey City, yester-

PLANT BLOWN UP; 100 MAY BE DEAD

Series of Explosions Wreck the Gillespie Shell-Loading Works at South Amboy.

LARGEST IN THE WORLD

Survivors Say That of 2,000 Men on Night Shift Hundreds Are Dead or Wounded.

MANY TONS OF TNT SET OFF

Plant Cost $18,000,000—Hope That Wrecked Buildings May Soon Be Replaced.

The shell-loading plant of T. A. Gillespie & Co., at Morgan, N. J., near South Amboy, said to be the largest shell-loading plant in the world, was partially destroyed with ... large loss of li... ...plosion...

FIRST EXPLOSION TERRIFIC

Earth Torn Away and Great Hole Filled with Blazing Debris.

The War Comes Home

The German agents made their way through the Jersey City railyards under the cover of darkness. Their leader was Heinrich Albert. He was a ruthless man with a command from the German Imperial Government burning in his heart: "Stop the supplies from getting to the British!"

He'd already had great success at throwing a monkey wrench into the American effort to send war supplies to the British, but tonight's work would be the payoff.

The United States was not yet in World War I in this midsummer of 1916, but sympathy for the Allies was growing. The Germans and the Allies were locked in bitter trench warfare across the length of Europe. Any advantage one side could gain might mean a breakthrough to victory.

The year before had seen a number of suspicious fires and explosions at American war supplies factories. The fire which destroyed the Roebling Steel Foundry in Trenton had been one of the worst. Others were almost as bad. Heinrich Albert, "commercial attache" at the German Embassy, was the man behind them all.

Tonight in the Lehigh Valley's Black Tom yard, freight cars loaded with more than two million pounds of high explosives were on the rails, and more was stored in barges in the river alongside.

The saboteurs prepared several piles of gasoline-soaked rags and wood, and dropped matches into them. They slipped away in the night as the fires grew and got to the boxcars.

At 2:08, very early in the morning of July 30, the first and most powerful explosion from Black Tom jarred the people of Jersey City and nearby New York awake. In this mighty blast more than a million dollars of damage was done in broken glass alone, as thousands of windows shattered in the business districts. The *New York Times* called the explosion "like the discharge of a great cannon," but there was more to come.

To add to the danger, smoking three-inch cannon shells were raining down on Jersey City and the area around it, along with flying metal and debris. Stunned people ran out into the streets, afraid the end of the world was at hand.

The hundreds of immigrants on Ellis Island, only a mile away from Black Tom, were getting an unexpected welcome to America. When the roof of the hospital caved in and the iron-bound door of the main administration building blew in "as if with a charge of dynamite," it was time to get off Ellis Island. A ferry took the terrified immigrants to the Battery in New York City.

The explosions lasted until the sun came up, some so close together they sounded as if cannon were firing like machine guns. The worst could be heard as far away as Camden and Philadelphia.

Though the Black Tom disaster did $20 million worth of damage, only three lives were lost, one a baby thrown from his crib in Jersey City. Some of the $20 million was recovered twenty-three years later from the German government.

Whether German spies were responsible for another great explosion some two years after Black Tom has never been proven.

The United States had been fighting in France for more than a year, and the end of the First World War was in sight. The T.A. Gillespie Loading Company was a major supplier of the American Army, turning out 30,000 cannon shells a day.

But the need to produce the shells became so vital that safety measures at the main plant on the outskirts of

Perth Amboy were relaxed. Company officials permitted a number of wooden storage sheds to be put up near the building where the TNT went into the artillery shells.

Though workers were searched when they came on duty for matches or anything else which might produce a spark, somehow a fire broke out in one of the sheds on the night of October 4, 1918.

A wind took it out of control and into the factory itself. The explosions began, and in three days killed 150 people. At the start, panicked workers trying to get out of the way of the blasts were cut down by shrapnel and flying glass. Those who made it as far as the fence around the factory were cruelly slashed by the barbed wire on top.

Perth Amboy became a combat zone, with exploding artillery shells falling on the city like a battlefield. It was a nightmare for the thousands trying to get out of town to safety. Looting of the damaged and abandoned houses began, and the National Guard had to be called out to stop it.

On the morning of October 5, one of the strongest of the explosions at the Gillespie Loading Company tore the doors off City Hall in New York City, miles away across the harbor. The ground all the way to the Jersey Shore shook as if an earthquake had hit.

Newspaper accounts quoted those close to the blast as saying they caused "flashes of yellow light as bright as day, and as the big flashes disappeared, the sky would be full of smaller explosions." The chunks of concrete and pieces of steel coming down after the big blasts were as large as rain barrels.

These two brief events brought a taste of the horror and destruction of the Great War in Europe home to New Jersey, making people here realize just how lucky they were.

A King in Bordentown

Napoleon Bonaparte was a great French general and emperor who conquered the armies of one European country after another. But after his defeat at the battle of Waterloo, Napoleon was finished. He was then sent to live the rest of his life on the small island of St. Helena and faded from history.

This final defeat naturally made things difficult for members of Napoleon's family, his brother Joseph especially. Napoleon had appointed Joseph to be the Spanish king.

Now the British were trying to hunt down all the Bonapartes, to make sure none of them would cause any more trouble. Joseph decided to flee to America to stay out of their hands. He'd settle "somewhere between New York and Philadelphia," and there he would be in a good position to get the latest news of France.

So in 1816 the brother of Napoleon Bonaparte, once king of Spain, came to New Jersey.

He picked Bordentown to live in and built a great estate there, at Point Breeze on the Delaware River. But one thing remained to be done. Bonaparte had to send a trusted agent back to Europe to dig up the gold and jewels he had buried there when things began to go wrong for his brother.

His agent, Maillard, made the dangerous trip to Switzerland, and, one jump ahead of spies and thieves who wanted the treasure for themselves, he rescued it for Bonaparte.

With the secret mission to Switzerland a success and his treasure safe in Bordentown, Joseph Bonaparte lived well on his great estate. He was a kind man and so well liked by his American neighbors that when his mansion burned down, they rescued his valuable jewels and possessions for him.

Joseph was away from the estate at the time and was so moved by this kindness that he often had parties for the people of Bordentown after his mansion was rebuilt. Anyone who needed work was welcome to cut firewood and do landscape work on the Bonaparte estate.

The mansion itself had all sorts of treasures: magnificent royal robes, some of which had belonged to the Emperor Napoleon himself, wonderful statues and vases, and beautiful oil paintings.

From all reports, Joseph Bonaparte was happy in America, or at least as happy as someone could be who had once been a king and now was not. He met a young Quaker woman, Annette Savage, and she became his good friend. He would often walk about his estate with friends and visitors, and was well spoken of by his servants.

In 1832 word came that Napoleon's son was ill. Joseph was needed in Europe. By the time he arrived in England, however, the son was dead. This put Joseph even closer in line to become the ruler of France.

But five years later he was back in Bordentown, spending his time supervising the estate work and boating on the Delaware. His two daughters urged him to come back to Europe and stay with them, and at the age of 71, he traveled to France, and then to Italy. After his long and eventful life was over, he was buried next to his brother, the Emperor, in Paris.

So for a time a king lived here in New Jersey, in a country which has no king, and he is remembered to this day in Bordentown.

They Took Giant Steps

The Black Doctor of Medford

James Still urged his horse on to something more than a walking pace as he realized how late it was getting. The sun was below the trees in the west, and he had a patient to see in the next town.

It was 1855. With his neat black suit and medical case, driving a fine wagon behind a lively horse, James Still had come a long way from his beginnings.

With not a day of formal medical training, this son of runaway slaves was now regarded by many in this section of Burlington County as something of a miracle man. Completely self-taught in everything from reading and figuring to medical lore, Still was a remarkable person.

It had all begun years earlier, when Still was a very small boy. A local physician, Dr. Fort, came to the family household to vaccinate the children. Young Still looked at the man with awe and decided then and there that he would become—somehow—a doctor, "riding around healing the sick and doing great miracles."

The next few years weren't easy ones for a man with a vision. James was "bound out" by his father to a neighbor for farm work. After his required three years of labor were up, Still went to work in a glue factory in Philadelphia. All the while he was reading and studying any medical texts he could get his hands on.

After his first wife died, James Still married again and set up housekeeping in Medford, farming four acres and tending livestock.

But the old dream was still strong, and he kept at his studies. He began to appreciate the healing qualities of medicinal plants and herbs. Still became what would be called today an "herbalist," gathering and selling nature's remedies to help a sick body heal itself.

Even though Still had no medical license, there was no law against his prescribing homemade remedies for the ailing. His practice grew as news of his cures spread about the county. Still was no mere salesman of potions—he was a healer of the sick.

James Still used such plants as sassafras, snakeroot, peppermint, and saffron to cure scrofula, tumors, and fevers. Area physicians, who had at first laughed at the "uneducated herbalist," came to respect and even admire James Still for his knowledge and skill.

Starting from nothing, Still achieved through the years a wide reputation as a healer and became the largest property owner in the area. He died in 1882, a fulfilled man.

Greater Love Has No Man—or Woman

The young nurse watched calmly as the deadly mosquito bit into her bare arm, making no effort to brush it away. She was part of a bold and dangerous experiment to find a cure for the dreaded tropical disease, Yellow Fever.

It was August 14, 1901, three years after the United States had fought Spain. In the Spanish-American War more American soldiers had died from the mosquito-borne disease, Yellow Fever, than had been killed by enemy bullets.

Clara Maas, the twenty-five year old nurse from Newark, knew about Yellow Fever. She had tended soldiers sick with the fever in 1898, during the war. She volunteered to serve again in 1901 and was now in Cuba with the Yellow Fever Commission headed by Dr. Walter Reed.

Reed and his associates had a theory about Yellow Fever. Though it was a deadly disease, they thought that if Yellow Fever could be detected at once and treated under ideal hospital conditions, it could be cured in almost every case.

But he needed people to test his idea. A call went out for volunteers willing to let themselves catch the disease in the name of science. Six people stepped forward, and Nurse Clara Maas was among them, the only woman.

She realized that allowing herself to be bitten by the Yellow Fever mosquito could mean her death. She'd already had a serious tropical fever in the Phillipines. It was a bad way to be sick.

Besides, the "controlled hospital conditions" theory of Dr. Reed's was just a theory—what if it didn't work?

These thoughts must have been going through Clara Maas' head that day in the Las Animas Hospital in Havana, as the disease mosquito infected her—but she didn't change her mind. She wasn't going to back out. If a cure could be found for this killer disease, the experiment would be worth it.

The six human guinea pigs were kept in a special isolation ward of the hospital and were watched closely by the Reed medical team.

For three days Clara Maas seemed to be bearing up well. Then, on the fourth day, she and two others in the test group began to feel the full effects of the dread disease.

She fought, but grew worse. The disease was too much for this heroic woman, and she began to sink.

On August 24th, at 6:30 p.m., ten days after voluntarily contracting Yellow Fever for the Reed Commission, Clara Maas died.

Three of the volunteers lived; three died. Why one and not another to live or die? No one knows what chance roll of the dice determines this, but we do know Clara Maas gave her life for her country and for her fellow Americans as surely as if she had fallen on the field of battle as a soldier.

The Judge Risks a Stomach Ache

The wise-looking judge stood on the steps of the Salem County Courthouse in front of a surprised crowd and reached down into the bushel basket at his feet.

People gasped as he bit into a ripe, juicy tomato and began chewing. The judge finished it and bent over for another. He didn't stop eating until he had emptied the basket.

Then, he came down and walked through the crowd, smiling and telling everyone that he felt fine.

But even if he'd ended up with a minor case of indigestion after too much of a good thing—the Jersey tomato—the people who were there that day watching him eat were afraid much worse was going to happen to this respected judge.

The year was 1820, and there were many odd beliefs around. One of the strangest was that the tomato, also called "the love apple," was deadly poison. It was thought by early Jerseyans that anyone rash enough to eat one could count on a quick, one-way trip to the graveyard.

Judge Robert Gibbon Johnson, among other people who had made a study of the tomato, realized this was nonsense. The tomato was a native American vegetable, and was healthful and delicious.

More, New Jersey and the tomato seemed made for each other. The tomato plant needs plenty of hot summer sun and warm, moist nights to grow well, though it is not fussy about rich soil.

Judge Johnson knew if he could get farmers to grow the tomato and people to eat it, this tasty vegetable could become a fine cash crop for New Jersey.

So Judge Johnson decided to take the tomato in hand

for a dramatic demonstration that the tomato had been "bad mouthed," and that, in fact, it was healthful, not harmful.

That was the reason for his unusual luncheon on the courthouse steps, and his plan worked. The farmers standing around watching and waiting for the judge to drop dead were almost convinced that day.

When the judge continued to show up at the Salem County Courthouse to hear cases after his tomato lunch, they realized that the bad reputation this vegetable had was nonsense.

The tomato caught on, and the "Jersey tomato" became known as the best which could come out of the ground. Just before the end of the nineteenth century, a young chemist employed by the Campbell Soup Company in Camden invented a way to condense tomato soup. The Jersey tomato began going around the world in cans.

Judge Johnson was right about this vegetable becoming a big cash crop for the Garden State. After more than 200,000 cross-breedings, the perfect tomato had been found, and the tomato crop in New Jersey eventually made more than $20 million annually for Jersey farmers.

And all because one man in the early days had the wit to separate the truth from nonsense, even though he might have ended up with a stomach-ache—or worse—doing it.

Chasing a Dream—and the Ballot

It's hard to believe now, but not so long ago women in this country had to fight for the right to vote.

And some other things are even tougher to swallow: back in the Dark Ages one of the serious debates among scholars was whether or not women had souls. As late as the first part of this century there were those who wondered if women were truly human!

That women be given the right to vote was regarded as something like treason by some, and madness by many.

With notions like these around, it's no wonder that early fighters in the struggle for women's rights thought of themselves as soldiers in a war.

One of the most effective battlers was Alice Paul, a tiny, frail Swarthmore College graduate from Moorestown—but a woman with a jaw that could set like iron.

After she finished college in 1905, Alice Paul left for England to study at the London School of Economics. One day she attended a rally for women's rights in London, and what she heard made sense to her.

Next week Alice Paul was in Norwich with some others in the movement, and she ended up arrested for disrupting a meeting at which Winston Churchill was speaking. She learned fast that ladylike politeness got her nowhere but ignored, and she became known for her rude and angry questioning of those opposing women's rights at public meetings. In fact, at one point she threw a chair through a window to get the attention of the Prime Minister, who was addressing a crowd!

By the time Alice Paul got back to the United States in 1912, she'd been jailed three times for her part in the struggle. The Quaker girl from Moorestown was a seasoned veteran.

She immediately joined the suffrage movement over here and somehow managed to organize a march of more than 5,000 women down Pennsylvania Avenue in Washington, D.C., one day before the inauguration of President Woodrow Wilson—just to let him know that women were watching.

Four years later things were bad. America was enthusiastically heading into World War I and had no time to listen to people like Alice Paul.

Nevertheless, she and her friends kept pressing. There were demonstrations which grew into near-riots, jailings, and beatings. During one arrest Alice Paul and another suffragette went on a hunger strike to dramatize the cause. They were force-fed, a bloody and painful process using a tube pushed up the nose into which food is poured, twice a day for a month.

Finally, in 1919, Congress passed the Nineteenth Amendment, which gave women the right to vote. Alice Paul and the National Woman's Party had won *half* the battle. The other half was to convince at least 36 of the 48 states to ratify the amendment, or it could not become law. Tennessee was the last of the 36 to do so, passing the Nineteenth Amendment by one vote. At last, women's voting rights were assured.

After the victory in the women's suffrage campaign, Alice Paul enrolled in law school and earned three law degrees. Her legal education made her realize that nothing less than "complete and full equality under the law" for women and everyone else here would make life complete in the United States.

She drafted an Equal Rights Amendment in clear and simple language, and it was introduced into every session of Congress for the next half century.

Though the ERA finally passed Congress in 1972, it did not have the good fortune of the voting rights amendment. Not enough states ratified it, and the Equal Rights Amendment did not become law. But ERA supporters have introduced the bill again, and vow to keep up the fight until it is won.

On August 26, 1970, thousands of women dressed in white paraded down Fifth Avenue in New York, to commemorate a similar march held fifty years earlier to celebrate the passage of the Nineteenth Amendment.

With them was the memory of all their sisters who had suffered humiliation, scorn, and hurt down the years for the cause of equality.

And right out front marched the indomitable spirit of Alice Paul, the Quaker girl "who didn't know how to give up."

Fighter Makes it to the Top
—After He's Over the Hill

On a July night in Pittsburgh the man from Merchant-ville won himself the world heavyweight boxing championship, and he earned it the hard way.

Jersey Joe Walcott had finally arrived. He'd come a long way from his days as a road worker, ice man, and shipbuilder. It had taken a long time, too.

For this championship fight with Ezzard Charles in 1951, Walcott's age was officially listed as 37. But Jersey Joe had been around for years. There were those who said his real age was well over 40. Even so, at 37 Walcott would have been the oldest man in history to hold the heavyweight championship.

And people said more. Those who had seen Jersey Joe's fight with Champion Joe Louis three and a half years earlier claimed that Walcott had actually won that fight also, though the decision went to Louis.

Jersey Joe, who at one time had been a sparring partner of Joe Louis, knocked the champion down twice in this fight. He was like a ghost in the ring—he was everywhere and nowhere, jabbing, parrying, bobbing and weaving. And there was always the threat of that left which could explode like dynamite with half a chance.

That was what had gotten Ezzard Charles. Walcott managed to work his way inside Charles' defenses and put him away with a massive left to the jaw. This was the knockout punch which catapulted Jersey Joe to the top after so many years of waiting and hoping.

The new world champion had been an on again, off again fighter for years. He'd left the ring—sometimes for years at a stretch—and then gone back to it so often that many thought he was washed up by 1945.

But that was when Walcott got hooked up with Camden fight promoter Felix Bocchicchio. The story goes that when Bocchicchio approached Walcott to talk him into a comeback, Walcott took the promoter down in the cellar of his house to show him an empty coal bin.

Bocchicchio promised to have it filled by morning, and also promised to put Jersey Joe on the payroll so that the immediate money worries of Joe and his family would be over.

Then two years later—the big fight with Joe Louis. Though the referee, Ruby Goldstein, voted for Walcott, the two ringside judges awarded the fight to Louis.

Louis knocked out Jersey Joe in the rematch, and then Ezzard Charles and Walcott took turns beating each other, with Walcott the final victor.

Then it was up-and-coming Rocky Marciano's turn to have a try at world champion Walcott. Walcott put Rocky to the canvas with his deadly left in the first round, but 12 rounds later the young challenger dropped Joe with a short right.

Eight months later and another Walcott-Marciano bout. This time it was clear that for the grand old man of boxing, whatever his age, the time had come to hang up the gloves. Marciano ended the fight in the first round with an uppercut and a right cross.

Whispers
from the
Woods

A Jersey Devil?

For centuries people have enjoyed scaring themselves silly with tales of ghosts and monsters. Especially around campfires, or when the lights are low, such things seem possible, and stories of Bigfoot and the Abominable Snowman have chilled many a listener.

Most places have their own legends about "things that go bump in the night," and New Jersey is no exception. In the dark shadows of the Pine Barrens, a million-acre stretch of forest in the southeastern part of the state, people have been talking for generations about the Jersey Devil.

This is supposedly a creature with the face of a horse, the body of a kangaroo, a forked tail, and huge bat-like wings.

The most popular legend says that the Jersey Devil was born in 1735, the thirteenth child of a woman named Mother Leeds. She'd become so tired of having children, it is whispered, that when she learned she was pregnant again, she told neighbors that she wished the devil would take her unborn child.

According to the story, this newborn baby appeared to be normal at first, but then changed into a horrible monster, as the women who had helped in his birth watched in terror. The monster baby's first meal was his own family, and immediately afterwards the Jersey Devil flew up the chimney with a horrible scream and started a 200-year career of terrifying the countryside.

For years, almost everything bad that happened in the Pine Barrens was blamed on the Jersey Devil. There were stories of cows going dry, crops failing, and dogs driven mad from barking: the Jersey Devil made them do it. There have been reports of farm animals killed by the creature, and, late on Saturday night, people making their way home through the forest have sworn they've seen him burn the tops off trees with his hot breath.

The Jersey Devil, to hear some tell it, has been seen walking along with a headless pirate, an unfortunate fellow left by Captain Kidd to guard buried treasure. At other times, he's been spotted hand in hand with a mermaid, and a ghostly girl dressed all in white.

Though there were now and again sightings of the creature, the Jersey Devil really got around during one amazing week in 1909.

Apparently the Jersey Devil got the urge to travel. He left his native Pine Barrens and wandered off to the west. He was first seen on Saturday night, January 16, in Woodbury by a man leaving a hotel, then up in Bristol, Pennsylvania in the early hours of the next morning.

"The thing was winged, and it hopped like a bird. Its voice was a horrible scream," reported shaken observers in Bristol as the Pine Barrens beastie roamed the streets of this waterfront town.

Next it was Burlington's turn to host the Jersey Devil, where people swore they saw what looked like "a two-legged cow with wings." Farmers began setting steel traps to catch the devilish creature, and posses of men with dogs tried to get on his trail.

But a couple of days later the Jersey Devil was reported in Gloucester, some miles to the south. Early in the morning on Tuesday, January 19, a paperhanger and his wife were awakened by a noise. On the roof of their shed, the Jersey Devil was doing a dance, and kept up the performance for ten minutes. There was no camera available to record the event, but the paperhanger was able to describe what he saw.

"It was about three feet and a half high, with a head

like a collie dog and a face like a horse. It had a long neck, wings about two feet long, and its back legs were like those of a crane, and it had horse's hooves. It walked on its back legs and held up two short front legs with paws on them."

After a tour of some neighboring towns, including Camden, Swedesboro, and Glassboro, the Jersey Devil's vacation ended and he was seen no more outside his home in the Pine Barrens.

The week of terror was a long time ago, but it seems the Jersey Devil is still around. Now and again he gets lonely and likes some human company, though he hasn't ventured out of the woods very often since 1909.

But a few years ago, in 1966, a poultry farmer near Batsto in the heart of the Pine Barrens awoke one morning to find his chickens and ducks savaged by an unknown night visitor. Two large watch dogs had also been killed and dragged hundreds of yards off in the bush.

State Police found an odd set of tracks at the chicken coops, leading off into the woods, but they were unable to determine whom the tracks belonged to. Was the Jersey Devil up to his old tricks?

White Stag in the Dusk

On the way from Evesham the stagecoach ran into a summer storm west of Thompson's Tavern, the stopover for the night on the trip from Philadelphia to the seashore.

In 1809 the only way to get anywhere, besides walking, was by horse or wagon. This journey to the shore—not much more than 50 miles—usually took a full two days. At the end of it, passengers were very glad to get out of the rough-riding stage.

But this time the journey looked as if it might take longer. The wind howled, the rain came down, and the sky got darker and darker.

The stage driver urged his team of horses on through the mud. He knew he had to reach Thompson's before nightfall, or risk an unpleasant and perhaps even dangerous night on the road. There were still robbers in these woods who waited for lonely travelers. He didn't want to have to rein up with a pistol in his face and have his passengers robbed.

The storm seemed to get even worse as the stage neared Quaker Bridge, a log bridge over the Batsto River. The driver was glad to see they had almost reached this bridge, because Thompson's Tavern was just east of the river on this same road.

Any minute now he would see the welcoming lights of the inn beyond the bridge, and there *was* a light through the heavy twilight, there ahead.

But the puzzled stagedriver saw that the light was on *this* side of Quaker Bridge, not at all where Thompson's Tavern was supposed to be, further on.

As the stage got closer to the bridge, the light got stronger—a pure white light—and the driver was amazed to see a huge white deer, a stag, in the middle of the strange brightness. He rubbed his eyes and peered through the gloom. It was still there—a light like the sun, and in the middle of it a white stag, pawing the ground, like no other animal he'd ever seen.

Suddenly the light disappeared, and the white stag with it.

The driver hauled back on his reins to stop his frightened horses and got down to take a look. The passengers were too afraid to get out of the stage, so he hurried forward alone.

Up ahead—when he got there—there was nothing at all and no sign that anything had been there.

But above the shrieking of the wind and the pounding of the summer rain, the coachman heard something else. It was the sound of rushing, tumbling water, almost like a waterfall.

It must be the Batsto, he thought, swollen with the rain. The driver walked a bit further down the muddy road, just to check.

A short way on he reached Quaker Bridge, or at least what was left of it. The stormy waters of the Batsto had ripped the bridge from its supports. Its tangled wreckage was scattered everywhere.

If the stage had thundered around the last turn to Quaker Bridge and across it, the coach, the driver, and all the passengers would have been thrown into the raging Batsto River, probably to drown.

And if the mysterious light and the white stag had not been there, this would have happened.

The story of the white stag is still told today, in the Quaker Bridge area of the Pine Barrens.

Witches in the Woods

Like others living close to nature and the land, the people of the Pine Barrens often tell stories of witches and ghosts. After all, this great woods of more than one million acres has plenty of elbow room for roaming ghosts and night-riding witches.

One of the most well known witches here, Peggy Clevenger, was said to be able to change herself into any sort of small animal she wished.

One day hunters chased a rabbit to her house and he jumped into the window. When the hunters' dog leapt up at the window, Peggy's face suddenly appeared behind it. The dog ran off yelping.

On another day, a woman was trying to get over a fence, but a big green lizard was on top of it and got in her way. She threw a stone at the lizard and hit it in the eye, and it disappeared. Next day the woman happened to see Peggy Clevenger and noticed that she had a black eye.

Witches were feared for casting "spells" on people. A victim would lose his appetite, feel tired all the time, or laugh for hours on end.

If a person suspected a witch had worked a spell on him, the remedy was to draw a picture of the witch and poke at it with a pin. The witch would supposedly feel the pin and call off the spell, knowing the game was up.

Witches would often come around to their neighbors' houses to try to borrow things. It was thought that if a witch had something belonging to someone else in her possession, she could easily work a spell on him or her. As a result, anyone suspected of witchcraft had a hard time asking for the loan of a cup of sugar.

Witches were also supposed to be able to walk up

walls and across ceilings if they felt up to it. However, if somebody saw a witch do this and said anything like, "You'll fall!" that's just what the witch would do.

Pine Barrens witches apparently enjoyed riding other people's horses at night, often to the point of exhaustion. A sign that witches had been night-riding an animal was a braided tail and mane—besides a very tired horse, of course.

Witches didn't like salt or horseshoes, both signs of good luck. A horseshoe nailed up over a doorway or a bag of salt hung there would keep a witch from coming into that house or barn, or so some people believed.

People in the Pine Barrens say they have seen a mysterious "man with a lantern" dressed in old fashioned clothes who walks along what once was a stagecoach trail in the woods. If anyone looks at him for too long a time, he disappears.

The man with a lantern is thought to be the ghost of someone who was murdered here almost 200 years ago, shot from ambush as he walked along with a lantern to light his way. This man, John Dobbs, was also believed by some to be "haunt" of a house built on a creek. Dobbs once lived there, and for years after his death strange sounds could be heard in the house in the dark of the night. It was so bad that for nearly 100 years after his death tenants refused to stay in the house for more than a few days.

One Pinesman recalls a chilling incident which occurred after he moved into a new cabin. Late one deep winter night he and his son were awakened by footsteps coming up to the door.

They could hear the snow squeak under the visitor's shoes, but he didn't knock or try to come in. Next morning when the man and his son checked for footprints in the snow by the door, they were surprised to find none.

The next night the visitor came again and stood outside the door. The two were frightened by now, but they kept quiet and looked out the window. They could see no shadow where a man was supposed to be. The mystery visitor, whoever or whatever, went away, again leaving no footprints. He didn't come again.

The Wizard with his
Head Between his Knees

Wizards are people who are supposed to have powers that the rest of us can only wonder at. There are some who think wizards can make water run uphill, cause clouds to appear in a clear sky, and soothe angry bulls.

Wizards are also popular in folk tales, and in the stories of most countries of the world, wizards pop up as often as princes who were once toads, scheming witches, and lonely maidens.

Long ago, just after the American Revolution, whispers began to go around in the New Jersey Pine Barrens of a man with strange powers. People claimed Jerry Munyhon was a wizard and could do things which couldn't be explained by ordinary means.

There was the time Jerry asked the owner of a bog iron furnace for a job. But the owner had heard of Munyhon and was afraid to hire someone who might be a wizard.

Jerry looked him in the eye and said, "Very well, if you won't hire me, I'll shut your furnace down," and almost as soon as he said this, clouds of black smoke began pouring out the furnace chimney. A great flock of crows had settled in the smokestack and were clogging it up.

At this the owner grew even more frightened and begged Jerry to set things right. After making the man promise to give him a job, Jerry called off the crows and the trouble was over.

The local merchants also came to know Munyhon. Before going into a store, Jerry would fill his pockets with clam shells. He'd pay for what he bought with silver coins out of these same pockets, but after he had gone, the storekeeper would find nothing but clam shells in his cash drawer.

Munyhon was thought to have a magic ax which could chop firewood by itself, and a walking stick able to run errands for him. He could charm cows into losing themselves in swamps, and then get them out with a wave of his hand—if their owners would pay him a fee.

But Munyhon's best trick was the way he could use his head. Once he asked a woodchopper's wife for a meal. When she refused, he made her dance until she was dizzy. Then he asked her to give him a haircut. She again refused and went off angrily to do some chores. When she returned, Munyhon was sitting in her kitchen with his head between his knees, cutting his own hair! By the time the excited woman raised an uproar, Jerry had his head back where it belonged and had left for the woods.

The Devil Strikes Out

Besides the legendary Jersey Devil, who regards the Pine Barrens as his own territory, there's another devil there too.

This is the fellow whose chief interest is trying to buy up peoples' souls. But the folks who live in the Pine Barrens, according to the stories, are too smart for him. He usually ends up empty-handed.

Once the devil met a poor woman who was out begging. She needed money to feed her three children, and the devil said he'd give it to her, as much as she wanted. All she had to do in return was promise him the first thing she tied up in the morning.

When the good woman told her husband about it, he realized she had made a deal with the devil. How to get out of it? Then he had an idea. He said to his wife, "When you get up tomorrow morning, instead of putting on your robe—and knotting the belt—just put on the clothes you're going to wear for the day."

"Then, tie a string around the cat's leg and put him out on the doorstep." The woman's husband knew that the devil was counting on his wife's putting on her robe first thing in the morning. If she did, and tied the robe's belt, she would go to the devil.

But the devil was gentleman enough to hold to his bargain. When he appeared next morning and saw the cat, he took him away and said nothing, and that was the end of it.

Another time an old woman named "Barefoot Betsy" fooled the devil also. Barefoot Betsy wanted very much to have the powers of a witch, but none of her charms or tricks would work.

Finally, she made a promise to the devil that if he

would allow her to perform three "miracles" in seven years, she would be his. He agreed, and she had her three miracles.

At the end of seven years the devil showed up to take Betsy below to his kingdom. Betsy asked him, "Will you wait until I put my shoes on?" He replied that he would, and Betsy told him, "Then I don't think I'll put them on."

And she never did put them on, summer or winter, from then on. She not only tricked the devil, she ended up with a nickname for the rest of her life.

In another incident the devil seemed content to wait also. A man's time had come, and the devil was there to take him away. Sammy, for that was the man's name, asked if the devil would mind waiting until the candle stub on the table burned down. The devil agreed, and Sammy immediately blew out the candle and put it in his pocket with a smile.

One Pinesman went into partnership with the devil, growing crops and raising livestock. When the harvest was in and the time came to divide up the corn, the devil asked his partner, Joe, how to do the sharing.

Joe said he'd be happy to have the middle, "And you can have the tops and bottoms." So Joe got the corn, and the devil got the stalks and roots.

When the hogs were slaughtered, Joe asked for all those with twisted tails, saying the devil could have those with straight tails. Of course there were no pigs with straight tails, so once again Joe ended up with the better part of the bargain.

After many other similar adventures with the devil in which Joe outwitted him every time, Joe grew old and died.

He was directed to the devil's kingdom, and knocked on the door. The devil asked, "Who's there?" Joe replied, "It's your old friend, Joe."

The devil remembered. "Well," he said, "my friend Joe, you can go right on. There's no room for you here." And that was how Joe got out of a warm reception.

The Sea Around Them

The New York

Copyright, 1934, by The New York Times Company.

NEW YORK, SUNDAY, SEPTEMBER 9,

Entered as Second-Class Matter.
Postoffice, New York. N. Y.

27,987.

s That's
int."

RO CASTLE BURNS OFF
ASBURY PARK; 250 AR
LISTED AS DEAD OR M

MANY BURNED IN CA

Rescue Liners Pick U
Craft Near By

*Four Large Vessels Pu
Circle Water With Coa
of the Saved Are*

Survivors Tell of Leaping
Into Sea to Escape Flames

*Many Sang and Prayed on Decks—Reluctant
Women Pushed Overboard or Into Boats
—Ship's Plates Red Hot.*

mes Cut Off Es
ourists Returr

Cruise to Cu

From north, east and south passenger
their courses yesterday to go at full spe
point off Shark River Inlet, above Sea Girt, N
Morro Castle with 318 passengers and a crew

Off Ambrose Light the Monarch of Ber
Savannah turned around and sped southwa
about twenty miles to the distressed ship. 1
miles, came the freighter Andrea S. Luckenbac
further away than the others, the President Cle
the night.

The S O S from the Morro Castle
was received by the Monarch and
the Savannah line vessel at about
the same time, 4:30 A. M. daylight
time. The Luckenbach ship had
been attracted by the sight of the
flames and radio confirmation that
the Morro Castle needed help came
from a land station.

Rescues Began in the Dark.

The sea was turning the color of
gun metal in a murky dawn when
the Monarch and the Savannah arrived to find that the Luckenbach
was already on the scene, as well
as several Coast Guard craft.

They came upon a scene of con-
fusion and horror. The liner was
blazing from B deck upward. On
the surface of the water were passengers and members of the crew
who had jumped.

The water was being combed by
the Coast Guard craft and two lifeboats from the Luckenbach. Four
of the lifeboats from the Morro
Castle had been successfully lowered, six on the port side having
been made inaccessible by the
flames

The rescuing ships stood by until
they could no longer be of service,
and then steamed for New York,
carrying in all, 157 survivors including at least forty members of the
Morro Castle's crew and one woman who was dead when taken from
the water.

Survivors of the Morro Castle,
the fire-swept liner yesterday,
and of panic.
Some of them told
the Morro Castle and swimming for
ing ashore or being picked up off the Jersey coas
to New York on the rescue vessels, told of being picked up from the
water.

Many told of being forced to jump into the sea
from the crowded decks when the approaching flames left them
Members of the

of them, on the
determined not
Captain Franc
off Ambrose Li
A. M. daylight
received an S.O.
Castle. He turn
and made all sp
ward the spot of
about twenty mi
the Morro Castle
anchored.

It was not ye
weather was squa
sea, as the Monar
The Andrea
freighter, of the L
was at least a half-
Morro Castle than
arch.

"I messaged the
Captain Francis a
message came back
be there in a half-hou
hour I messaged
want assistance.'
came back, 'Yes

'We reached the M
about 7:30 A. M. It
daylight From four
away we could see ti
glare of light on the
came within 100 yards
Castle and lowered fou
under the command o
tain Leslie Banyard
thirty-one persons. W
mainly out of the wa
the poop deck.

ral women, were in the water for
as long as seven hours. Several
were picked up by Coast Guard
boats less than 100 yards from the
beach at Sea Girt.

The outstanding swimming feat
was that of Antonio Mais, 20, a
Cuban mess boy. He swam from
ship to shore without a life belt
and was rescued from the surf off
Sea Girt just as he collapsed. However, several of the passengers
aided by life belts, made their wa
through the ocean from the burnin
ship to the Jersey coast.

When the rescue ships arr
here late yesterday afternoon
piers were thronged with an
of joyous relatives and friends

A few of the passengers
of the members of the
had landed in Jersey
to the city during the
train, the passenger
Hotel New York
the Seamen's Chu
to their homes

Docter Awake
Dr. Charles C
lyn, one of the
and lyn, in vivid story of
aided greatly in he had been
s for passengers the Long Branc
to jump into the T Co
stood at least some Brooklyn
river

List of Victims
in Sea Disaster
and Survivors

*Passengers and member s of the
crew reported accounted for, un-
injured or missing, together with a
list of the identified dead in the
burning of the Ward liner Morro
Castle, on the basis of the latest
available information, were as fol-
lows:*

SURVIVORS.

Passengers.

ADAMS, JANE, Point Pleasant,
N. J.; injured, shock and sub-
mersion.
AGUIAR, VAL, Las Vegas, Vene-
zuela.
ARNETH, PAUL, Brooklyn.
ASCHOFF, THORP H., 150-15
Stoneford Avenue, Flushing,
Queens.
ATICELLO, MARCO, Brooklyn.
ASCHOFF, Mrs. T. H.; same ad-
dress.
BARSTEAD, LLOYD C., 1,891 Har-
rison Avenue, Bronx.
BARSTEAD, Mrs.; same address.
BECK, Miss EMILY C., Philadel-
phia.
BEACH, AGNES, 205 East Seven-
Street.

The Ship on the Beach

September, 1934, and a four-year old passenger liner of the Ward Line, the *Morro Castle*, was on its way back to New York after a trip to Havana, Cuba.

It was the last night of the pleasure cruise, but all was not well. The Captain, Robert R. Wilmott, had died of a heart attack the day before, and a storm of hurricane strength was following the ship up from the south. The *Morro Castle* was undermanned by a crew which complained of poor food and bad working conditions. A number of the crew had been involved in smuggling incidents on the ship's previous Cuba runs.

Then, somehow a fire broke out in a storage locker in the writing room, just behind the main lounge. Time was lost in detecting the fire, and when the crew finally began to fight it, flames had spread across to the ship's library.

It was just before 3:00 a.m. and most of the passengers were asleep as the crew tried frantically to put out what had now become a raging, ship-killing fire.

But it got away from them after an explosion spread the flames all over the midsection of the ship. The acting captain, William F. Warms, tried to turn the *Morro Castle* toward the New Jersey coast only a few miles away, but by this time the fire had eaten through the ship's steering controls. The men in the engine room had to leave their stations or be burned to death, and the once sleek luxury liner rapidly became a burning, drifting hulk, pushed along by 35 mile per hour winds.

Passengers began to awake to find smoke and flames everywhere. The electrical wiring had burned through, and where there was not fire, there was darkness. The ship's whistle blew, a signal to stand by the boats.

People were already trying to get away from the fire and smoke, squeezing themselves through eighteen-inch portholes to drop to the sea. Some slept through all the alarms until it was too late.

An SOS had been sent by the *Morro Castle* radio operator, and ships were on their way to help. They began arriving just after 4:00 a.m. and launched their lifeboats to pick up passengers in the water. Rescuers were horrified at what they could see of the *Morro Castle:* "she was a ball of flame amidships . . . there were two tall towers of flame . . . horrible screaming."

In the panic to get away, lifeboats from the *Morro Castle* left the ship half empty, and almost half a dozen ship's boats on the port side were not launched at all. The fire was blistering the feet of those still on deck, forcing them to jump, and many had no lifejackets. A man with a pistol held off another who tried to take his wife's place in a lifeboat. A man in the water in a lifejacket pushed away an exhausted passenger who wanted to cling to him to rest for a moment. The man went under immediately. A young college student, holding up a little boy, took the lifejacket off a dead woman and used it to save both of them.

The seas were high, with waves ranging up to ten feet and more in the gale. Those without lifejackets were holding on to deck chairs, stray oars, anything they could get their hands on. Many were giving up. Out of a total of 549 passengers and crew aboard the *Morro Castle* for the fall pleasure cruise, 135 would lose their lives this dreadful night.

By now those on shore had seen the flames, and word of the disaster quickly spread all along the central New Jersey coast. People in places such as Spring Lake, Sea Girt, Manasquan, and Belmar turned out to help as the survivors and lifeboats began coming ashore. They brought dry clothing, blankets, hot drinks, and provided first aid and emergency shelter.

All morning long the living and the dead came ashore on the sandy beaches. And then the *Morro Castle* herself, completely gutted by fire and still aflame, her dead captain still lying in his stateroom, started to stand in to shore.

Pushed by a strong northeast wind, the *Morro Castle* edged toward the seaside resort of Asbury Park. The ship grounded just opposite Convention Hall, 200 feet from shore. It was like "a ghost coming in from the night," in the words of one awestruck witness.

It was six months before the burned out hulk of "one of the world's safest ships" would be pulled off the beach and towed away to be broken up for scrap.

"Get Out—It's a Hurricane"

New Jersey is generally free from weather disasters such as tornados and "twisters" which often hit other areas of the country. But this state has a long coastline, and now and again New Jersey plays host to unwelcome visitors—hurricanes.

Hurricanes are massive storms which begin as weather disturbances, usually in the south Atlantic. The name itself comes from a Spanish word, "Huracan," which may in turn have come from a word for "storm god" in an earlier language.

No one has ever seen the birth of a hurricane. We do know, however, that a hurricane starts as an area of low air pressure. Somehow this low attracts circling winds. If other conditions are present, including the jet stream dipping closer to earth, what begins as a minor tropical storm can be molded into a dreadful force.

What's hard for the weather experts is to predict just where a hurricane will go once it's on the move. Many hurricanes head west to the Gulf Coast, while others come ashore in Florida and wear themselves out inland. Some, though, go up the coast and reach as far north as New England. Almost a dozen have struck New Jersey within living memory, some causing terrible damage and even death.

What's it like to actually be in a hurricane? Imagine a late summer or early fall day at the shore, the hurricane season. The barometer, an instrument which measures air pressure, slowly begins to drop. The sun goes down red, in a sky with high, trailing clouds in it. The ocean has a heavy rise and fall. Things are starting to feel odd, somehow.

Late that night a hot breeze starts up and continues

into morning. The barometer has fallen another inch by daybreak and is still going down. The wind soon begins to gust, and from far off, where the sky is dark, there's a sound of rain. The gulls and sandpipers are flying every which way, as though they're afraid of something.

A couple of hours later the hurricane is here and it's like the end of the world. The sky is dark as night, the wind is building to a howl, trees are bending and breaking, and anything left outside is banging up against houses or rolling down the streets. The shore has become a nightmare of great wind, blackness, and the fearsome roar of the sea.

The wind is up to close to one hundred miles an hour now, and it's like being inside a railroad tunnel with an express train. It's taking the roofs off houses—there goes one, tearing off in big squares of plywood.

A surge of crazy green and white water comes over the dunes and runs down the street. There's another, and another, as the hurricane's storm surge hits. This is a great dome of water, miles wide, with terrible waves on top. It's the most destructive thing about a hurricane, aside from the wind.

The streets are starting to flood with seawater, and a couple of houses near the beach are twisting away from their foundations. One home right on the oceanfront has been lifted up and carried halfway down the block, where it's breaking up. Boats, beach chairs, wooden walkways—cars even—are being tossed about by the wind and water.

Then, almost as if somebody pulled a switch, the wind and rain stop and the sky clears. Now there's only the terrible sound of the sea. The "eye" of the hurricane has arrived. This is the calm center around which the great winds of the storm move.

For perhaps twenty minutes there will be no storm.

Now is the time to get things secured, leave low lying areas, get across the bay to safety.

But the eye lingers only briefly. A sound like a mountain avalanche can be heard in the distance. The storm is once again on the move, and the bad dream is coming back.

The cycle of great wind, rain like hail, the sea spilling over the dunes and bulkheads as the second storm surge hits, is all here again.

By evening the hurricane moves northeasterly and off the coast, to blow itself out at sea. Dazed people come out of their houses and emergency shelters to assess the damage and begin the clean-up.

Killer Shark on the Loose

What came to be known as "The New Jersey Shark Attack" began without warning one hot day during the summer of 1916 in the surf at Beach Haven.

A large fish went after Charles Vansant as he was swimming at the Center Street beach. After he was struck, a "human chain" of bathers was formed to get the badly bleeding young man ashore. People at the scene said the fish which took most of Vansant's leg off was "blue-grey and almost ten feet long."

Though Vansant died that night from shock and loss of blood, most thought the attack was a freak occurrence not likely to happen again.

But they were wrong. Five days later, at a seaside resort some miles to the north of Beach Haven, Spring Lake, another swimmer was attacked just beyond the breakers. Charles Bruder, a bellboy at a shorefront hotel, lost both his legs in the sudden attack and died before lifeguards could get him ashore in their boat.

Now the entire coast was in an uproar. There was talk of putting up protective wire netting around some of the resort beaches, but people were so frightened they were staying away from the ocean no matter what.

And the killer shark was not finished yet. Less than one week after the second attack, the shark was in Raritan Bay and on his way to the town of Matawan. A retired sea captain spotted the shadowy figure of the great fish as its made it way up the narrow creek to the town— and its last victims.

Though the alarm was immediately given, a 12-year old boy, Lester Stilwell, scoffed at the idea that a killer shark could be this far up an inland creek so far away from the ocean. He was pulled under while swimming with friends, and was not seen alive again.

When Stilwell's companions ran screaming through Matawan to report what had happened, Stanley Fisher dived into the water to save him. He actually succeeded in reaching the boy's body and was starting for shore, when he too was attacked and fatally injured.

Hundreds of people lined the banks of Matawan Creek armed with rifles and shotguns, shooting at everything and anything which could by any stretch of the imagination be the shark.

Despite this, on its way downstream to Raritan Bay the shark managed to make a pass at a boy pulling himself out of the water on a ladder, and badly mauled his leg.

Authorities still did not know if a single shark was doing all the damage—a "rogue shark"—or whether there was a pack of sharks involved, but on the morning of July 14th, two days after the Matawan Creek attacks, it was all over.

A New Yorker, Michael Schliesser, hooked an eight-foot white shark, the most dangerous kind of shark in the ocean and the one known as "the man eater," and boated it after a terrific struggle. Was this shark the killer, and, if so, was he the only one? There was no real answer to these questions, but after Schliesser's shark was caught, the attacks stopped. The people of the Jersey Shore could breathe easier.

They Still Call It
"The Great March Storm"

The straining truck barely made it through the raging water and howling winds to the trailer park at Holgate, on the south end of Long Beach Island.

Coast Guardsmen aboard picked up the seven people still there and started back to the station in Beach Haven. But a surge of waves spilling over the dunes hit the truck hard. It went over, dumping everyone into the icy water.

"Link up your arms, stay together!" was the order given by the driver and his crew to the terrified passengers. The Coast Guardsmen struggled in the fiercely rolling surf to form a human chain with their passengers and help them scramble back to safety.

But the chain of linked arms broke, and two screaming people were carried away by the sea. Weeks later their bodies would be found 30 miles to the south.

Just a few days ago it had been an ordinary early spring on the Jersey coast. People were getting ready for summer, with no idea what was in store for them this fateful March.

The winter of '61–'62 hadn't been bad—some light snow and the usual cold winds from the northwest blowing for weeks at a stretch—but nothing unexpected.

Then the elements ganged up on the New Jersey shore. Two huge storm areas came together east of the coast and hung there. And a full moon was boosting tides to their peak.

The result was a 48-hour storm which brought winds up to 70 miles an hour, raging seas which covered the shoreline in many places, and giant waves which broke over dunes and bulkheads. Houses were battered into

105

hulks, cars disappeared into the bay, and the wreckage of anything which tried to stand against the storm was everywhere.

The storm did $80 million worth of damage on the coast. Seven people, including a police chief on a rescue mission, died in what came to be known as "The Great March Storm."

It roared in on the morning of March 6, catching shore residents completely off guard. The wind came first, then the high water raging up and over the beaches into the streets.

The next day was when the giant waves started coming ashore, making it impossible to tell where the land ended and the sea began. The wind kept up to gale force for more than 48 hours, and the temperatures stayed in the thirties. Snow came along with the storm, but there was no dry ground for it to settle on.

People took shelter in Coast Guard stations and fire houses up and down the coast, their homes broken up by wind and water—in many cases just minutes after they fled them.

Helicopters flew between the mainland and the shore, bringing off people as fast as they could be gotten aboard. A Navy destroyer, adrift and rudderless, was blown aground near Beach Haven. Another man died getting the ship off the sand.

The statistics for Long Beach Island alone tell some of the story: Long Beach Township lost 300 homes, Ship Bottom, 60. Half the houses in Harvey Cedars were destroyed. In many cases, the foundations of these lost homes could not even be located.

In Atlantic City, the world famous Steel Pier had its entire midsection torn away by the wind and water. Loveland Tower in Manasquan was blown down.

The storm cut completely through Long Beach Island,

creating three new "inlets" from the ocean to the bay. One of these was a quarter of a mile wide and a dozen feet deep.

When the storm finally passed and the wind and sea grew calm, the New Jersey shore looked as if a war had been fought there. Sixteen people were dead and a huge amount of damage was done. And the Great March Storm wasn't even a hurricane!

"We're Going Down!"

The *Hindenburg* disaster at Lakehurst in May, 1937 is well known. The *Hindenburg* was a German airship, which had crossed the Atlantic many times, carrying passengers and mail. Airships of the Zeppelin Company had been flying for years and had a good safety record.

Nevertheless, something went wrong with the *Hindenburg* as it arrived at Lakehurst on the way in from Europe. A fire broke out, then an explosion. The airship fell to earth, killing 35 of those on board.

But another airship disaster off the coast of New Jersey is not so well known: the crash of the *Akron* four years earlier. The *Akron* had been built for the U.S. Navy and used the gas, helium, to make it float. It was nearly six times as long as it was wide. There were living quarters for the crew inside the actual airship, beside the cabin which was suspended from the main body. The *Akron* even had storage space for four or five airplanes, which could be launched while the airship was in flight. This airship was built with care and precision and was thought at the time to be one of the most perfect in the skies.

On an April day in 1933 the *Akron* took off from its base at Lakehurst for a flight up the New England coast. The weather was not good. A large cold front was coming in from the west, and thunderstorms were moving up from Washington. There was static electricity in the air, and fog began to roll in over Lakehurst.

But the flight went on. To stay out of the way of the storms, though, the airship would change its route and fly inland at first, then come around in a half circle over New England.

The storm was already ahead of the *Akron*, and by the time the airship got to Philadelphia it was so bad the captain decided to get away from it and head back over the ocean.

The *Akron* steered to the northeast, and by ten o'clock that evening had crossed the coast. An hour later there was lightning all around the ship, and compasses and radio direction finding equipment were useless. The crew did not even know for sure how far they were above the water.

Just past midnight, 35 miles out in the Atlantic off Barnegat Light, the *Akron* ran into an air pocket which dropped her hundreds of feet. It was almost as if the ship had fallen into a hole in the sky. The *Akron* went down to 700 feet. A great swirling mass of cold air shook the airship, and it dropped again.

The captain didn't know it, but his ship was dangerously close to the water. As the pilot lifted the nose of the airship to gain altitude, the ship's tail dipped into the sea, and was ripped off. The end was near for the *Akron*. Great black waves burst through the windows of the control car. A sudden cross wind pushed the bottom of the airship into the water, and the *Akron* was split apart by tons of seawater pouring into her.

There was no lifesaving gear aboard, and the Atlantic was bitterly cold. By the time rescuers reached the scene of the crash, only three men of the crew of 76 were pulled alive from the waves.

Silver from the Sea

A three day storm from the northeast had just blown itself out along the Jersey coast. The wind this December had swung around to the west now, and the sky was clearing.

It was not a day to go to the beach, but a man was walking along the south end of Long Beach Island, dressed in a heavy parka and wool cap. His eyes were on the sand at his feet, as if he were looking for something.

But he didn't find anything, at least for a while. Then he spotted something and quickly bent to pick it up. Rubbing sand and salt crust away from the object, he held it up in the weak winter sunlight.

It was a silver coin, minted long ago in 1772, and it was about the size of a half dollar. The coin had the picture of a king on it, "Carolus IIII," according to the lettering under it. The other side had a royal shield on it. More polishing brought up the shine, and the sun gleamed off the eye of the king.

It was a Spanish silver coin, and it was what this beach walker had been looking for. The day had been a success—he had found a "piece of four," a coin in use all over the known world centuries ago, and one worth real money today. "Pieces of eight," the larger Spanish coin the size of an American silver dollar, can be worth hundreds of dollars.

People have been picking up Spanish coins on Long Beach Island for as long as anyone can remember. They wash up on the beach after fall and winter northeast storms, just waiting for those with the eyes to see them, and there are islanders with cigarboxes full of them, all the way from the tiny piece of two up to the eight, a bit of silver worth a drop of blood in the New World of the 18th century.

But where do they come from, and how is it they appear only after heavy storms from the northeast?

There are many theories, but coin hunters believe a ship—what is called a "treasure trove"—lies sunken somewhere close offshore. When the waves and current are disturbed by northerly storms, the sunken ship gives up some of its treasure, a little at a time.

It could be the *Sally*, which went down off Long Beach Island in 1768, or the *Betsy*, which sank ten years later. Another *Betsy* sank in 1791, and the *Manchester* in 1793. And dozens of other ships since then were driven into the shallow waters around Long Beach Island and knocked to pieces by howling storms.

Or the treasure could be coming from somewhere on the island itself. Two hundred years ago, when Long Beach Island was wider, treasure might have been buried on the beach. That spot might be located out beyond the breakers now.

A curious incident at Little Egg Harbor would seem to make one believe there might be treasure on the island. Almost 100 years ago, two men came ashore from a ship anchored out from the beach. They asked at the Egg Harbor Life Saving Station about the location of some landmarks, then they disappeared.

Next morning, lookouts at the station saw the men digging near a big cedar tree. The excited lifesavers ran out to see what was happening, but by the time they got there the men had dragged a heavy chest to their boat and were rowing back to their ship. In the hole they left behind were a rusty cutlass and a scattering of silver coins.

Did they get it all? No one really knows, but one thing is certain—the Spanish silver coins of Long Beach Island keep coming in.